PASTORAL POETRY SERIES
POETRY FOR THOUGHT 2
A JOURNEY WITHIN
DERRICK STEPHENS

PASTORAL POETRY SERIES

POETRY FOR THOUGHT 2

A Journey Within

Derrick Stephens

Christian Publishing House
Cambridge, Ohio

Unless otherwise stated, Scripture quotations are from Updated American Standard Version (UASV) Copyright © **2021** by Christian Publishing House

POETRY FOR THOUGHT 2: A Journey Within by Derrick Stephens

ISBN-13: **9798595583930**

"Acknowledgement is made to *Crossroads – December 2020,* in which **A Festive Feel** appeared."

POETRY FOR
THOUGHT 2
A JOURNEY WITHIN

Table of Contents

Dedication

This book is dedicated to God,
And his son Jesus too.
To the family and friends, I love,
And of course, dear reader, you.

Thanks to Ed,
And the CPH "gang,"
For letting me climb back in the ring,
To don the gloves and bang.

Thanks to my wife,
Who never, says never.
The one who pledged to join this journey,
Always and forever.

Introduction

This is an exploration for inspiration,
Where feeling and destination, you decide.
This is Poetry for Thought two, and it's asking you.
To journey within and discover what abides.

This is a quest to find the best,
In yourself and those you love.
An adventure through time, and experiences that
define,
While led through loss, by God above.

This is a mission with a proposition,
To laugh and to give,
A journey within, that will only begin,
When we learn to live.

CHAPTER 1

LIFE IS MEANT FOR LIVING

The "Ville" on the "Hill"

Life is easy, laid back and breezy,
Living on this hill,
Smiles are shown and nicknames are known,
Living in the "ville."

You find a face you know, wherever you go,
Walking through the "ville,"
Where cars honk "hi," to friends they pass by,
On the streets of this hill.

From Chestnut Street to Main, Victorian structures reign,
Holding their charm still.
From the rail depot to the museum, we all love to see them,
Preserving history on this hill.

Church bells ring, and pumpkins are crowned King,
Festively in the "ville,"
With scenes that set our souls on fire,
And make our senses thrill.

BNV rocks, and we cheer for "Shamrocks,"
Spiritedly in the "ville,"
Folks help in a pinch, and tales are told on a "liar's bench,"
Warmly on this hill.

We stroll through the park, and its beauty is stark,
In admiration, in the "ville,"
Sitting by the lake, peace is yours to make,

Taking it easy on this hill.

There's no real surprise, you read it in the Enterprise,
Weekly in the "ville,"
Because everyone knows, how everything goes,
When living on this hill.

You rarely wear a frown, while in this town,
Living and enjoying, God's free will,
It's the place I call home, where my seeds are sown,
Welcome to Barnesville.

Ascension

When I conquer life's mountain,
Reaching its peak,
Will I lookback upon what was overcome;
Or dwell on moments, when the conquest seemed
bleak.

When I stand on life's summit,
Hoping to relish;
Will I realize, my trek has been amazing;
Or feel the need to embellish?

When I take the top,
Shouting I'm victorious,
Will I remember, who got me there;
Or boast how I am glorious?

Will I ascend above?
Listening for the call,
Will my life be found, eternally great;
Or end up Earthly small?

The Carousel

We start off timid,
As life goes 'round.
Life flies by,
As we live through its ups and downs.

Enjoy your ride,
Until your feet hit the ground.
Treasure each day,
Because, life's carousel only goes once around.

Questions of Life

They say, "a house divided,
Cannot stand."
And if "it takes a village to raise a child,"
Shouldn't we lend a helping hand?

They say that "love,
Can conquer all."
And if we can "roll with life's punches,"
Shouldn't we? Since "pride comes before we fall."

They say that "time,
Can heal all wounds."
And if we're told to "face the music,"
Wouldn't it sound better if our heart was attuned?

They say "misery loves company,"
So, don't pull up a chair.
And if life is filled with "silver linings,"
Shouldn't we be searching for their glare?

A Novel Approach

The book of life, is sharp like a knife,
Its words are etched as you go;
Line by line, it conveys your voyage in rhyme,
With your heart and soul in toe.

It states the stories of your glories,
Spotlights the moments, when you take the stage;
From floating on youth's fountain, to climbing time's
mountain,
Then you turn the page.

To tell the tale, of how you fail,
You write about wrongs, and morals you learn;
The mistakes you make, and missteps you take,
To share the wisdom, you have earned.

This is your novel, whose approach is novel,
Because everyone's book is unique;
Its signature is signed, by what you leave behind,
Defined in your technique.

If Life is What You Make

If life is what you make,
What will you create,
Will it be a loving memory;
Or a scar carved from hate?

If decision is a choice,
What will you choose?
Will you make sacrifices;
Or be afraid to lose?

If time is uncertain,
What can be known?
Will you read the directions to heaven;
Or get lost on your own?

If life is what you make,
What will you create?
Will it be a home in hell;
Or an entrance, through the straight and narrow gate?

A Taste for Living

Life can put a lot on your plate,
Making your stomach sore.
Life can also leave you hungry,
Hankering for more.

There are times, we want sympathy,
But drama we've given birth;
This is when we have a cow,
And milk it for all it's worth.

There are times, we crave fun,
And we hope our plates are jammed;
This is when we pig out,
And we become a ham.

There are times, we thirst for knowledge,
Till everything, we think we know;
This is when we eat humble pie,
Followed by some crow.

There are times, we're starved for affection,
And love's rose becomes thorny;
This is when flattery will get us everywhere,
Even if it is corny.

There are times, we've had our fill of life,
And all its grief;
This is when everyone else is full of it too
Because we've got a beef.

There are times, we're hungry for change,

And we get a little bold;
This is when we talk turkey,
Then we quit it cold.

Life can overfill you,
If you eat all it's giving;
But it can taste so much better,
If you only consume living.

Learn to Discern

This morning I awoke, and to the silence I spoke,
Saying, today I want to return;
To the better side of me, who I want to be,
Please God, help me to discern.

I headed to my car, but I didn't make it far;
When I saw my new neighbor, who can be vile.
But I threw up my hand and waved, then suddenly,
his face caved.
And wait, was that a smile?

On my way to work, I got a call from my boss, "the
jerk;"
Who asked me to work over, and I thought, why?
But as I told him I would; suddenly, his voice didn't
sound too good;
Was he going to cry?

The time dragged on, and all day, the boss was gone;
I wondered, where did he go to?
Till I heard Rose, from the elevator, and before it
closed;
She whispers, "Thank you."

So, finally it's time to punch out, and there's no doubt;
This has been a perplexing day.
Till the boss sends a text, and I think, what's next?
And in my office, he asks me to stay.

Then comes a knock on my door, and I groan,
thinking, "no more."

When in walks my boss, Rose and my neighbor.
They're all grinning at me, but the reason, I can't see.
Till my neighbor speaks, saying, "you did me a favor."

"You see I have cancer, and I didn't find an answer.
So, I decided to take my life.
Until I saw your hand, your smile, that made me
understand;
People care, if I overcome this strife."

"So, thank you for being nice, and thinking twice;
To say hello, to someone you didn't know.
You made me think, stopped me at the brink;
By the way, my name is Joe."

Then with tears in his eyes, my boss began to cry,
Saying, "you saved my boy."
Then Rose spoke too, and said, "I couldn't get through;
But you gave me back my love and joy."

We embraced and said our goodbyes, as I let out a
sigh;
Saying, "how did I do that?" to a silent room.
I guess God, helped me return and to discern.
My better side I assume.

Forgive and Live

This is the day, that I say,
I'm letting go,
Of this angry state, and all the weight,
To allow a smile to show.

This is the day, that I convey,
I will change.
How I feel, parts of me I seal,
Today, I rearrange.

This is the day, I do it another way,
Begin caring again.
Open my heart and allow it to start,
Forgiving other's sins.

This is the day, I wipe away,
All those tears,
That refused to fall, like it was a law,
Today, I make up for lost years.

This is the day, that I pray,
I am reborn.
From the life I've led, the things I've said,
Where my soul is no longer torn.

Undressed

In this life,
I must confess,
It's hard to remain decent,
When we all obsess to undress.

When anger sets in, we feel obligated to show some
skin,
But not to turn and cough.
No, when we're hot under the collar and ready to
holler,
It's those gloves that are coming off.

When we're ambitious for a life that's prestigious;
Motivation and excitement, we must bring.
So, we prepare, and strip our heads bare,
As we "toss our hat in the ring."

When we're surprised with affection in our eyes,
We're "head over heels in love," somehow.
But instead of taking a seat, we're "swept off our feet,"
And our socks are knocked off. WOW!

When we're generous and empathy centers us,
The needs of others keep us on track;
And with our deeds, we plant seeds,
As we're known for "giving the shirt off our back."

When we're not ready, our steps are unsteady;
And we're clumsy like a clown;
But woe, when we're unaware, our ignorance is left
bare,

As we're "caught with our pants down."

Yes, in this life,
I must confess;
That it's hard to stay decent,
When life demands that we undress.

CHAPTER 2

LOVE IS BETTER WITH GIVING

Undefined

What is love?
A quest we all must ask.
Is it a feeling that only has meaning;
If you put it to task?

Is it an emotion,
Discovered on your own?
Can sympathy or empathy,
Display it when shown?

Is it defined in desire?
Appeal or attraction?
Can it be expressed in yearning or burning?
Revealed in reaction?

What is love?
Is it joy or inspiration?
Can it be explained, or truly proclaimed;
As respect or admiration?

Can love be honest in peace;
Or is love only fair in war?
Can love be all of these;
All of these and more?

Sea of We

This is the tale, after we set sail,
Casting off from those "I do's."
With the wind at our back, and love securely packed,
We plot out; how can we lose?

So, we sail along, singing our merry song;
Till the waves ahead become a little choppy.
We correct our course, of course,
But it wasn't perfect, perhaps even sloppy.

Then comes the angry storms, and we try to perform;
Anything, to save our ship.
We fight the raging rain, but it all seems in vain.
We feel like we're losing our grip.

But we batten down the hatches, and navigate through
other patches;
Finding the depths of life are not too great.
When sailing on life's sea, there's nowhere better to be,
Then with your first mate.

Family Portrait

Beyond the present,
To the echoes of time;
I remember a smiling face,
That blissfully was mine.

Through the shining glass,
Reflection is clear;
A living memory is over there,
And, I'm out here.

I can smell that moment,
Feel that day's breeze on my skin;
See those who shared that time,
If only I could hear them again.

I recall all the emotions,
Held inside this frame;
Where a family's soul, love, and goals,
Were captured and contained.

I place this portrait back now,
On the shelf that holds my heart;
Wondering why moments aren't truly appreciated,
Till time sets us apart.

Together

For me and you,
It's hand in hand.
Through fears, and years,
Together, we'll stand.

For me and you,
It's heart to heart.
Stories shared, struggles bared,
Together, not apart.

For me and you,
It's eye to eye.
Faith driven, trust given,
Together, no lies.

For me and you,
It's step for step.
Joined in fate, to heaven's gate,
Together, eternally kept.

Always and Forever

This is to a mate, that has shared my fate,
Since the moment we said I will;
Keep you in my heart, and deny life from tearing us
apart,
Love you always and forever still.

From the best days to the worst, I pledge to put you
first,
Ahead of myself, where you belong to be.
So, everything we do, we'll think as two,
Then life will add up to true unity.

Till death sets us a drift, I'll try to be swift,
To be at your side, and let you know;
That a love that always gives, is one that forever lives,
Wherever we may go.

The Tapestry

Love is not manufactured, though it can be fractured.
When it comes from the heart;
Love is blind, but it still manages to find,
A way if it is destined from the start.

Love cannot be bought, nor can it be taught,
When it already knows what it wants.
Love is not always inclusive, but can be elusive,
So, it feels the thrill of the hunt.

Love is a mystery, but with a personal history;
It's understood, yet unknown.
Love cannot be explained, but is undeniably
contained;
Within all who've lived, it's sown.

Treasure Map

Family is a treasure,
That I pray all will find.
But what's contained in its splendor,
I'll try to explain, in this map I leave behind.

A father who is patient,
Who's concerned and cares.
One who's your friend, and your hero,
Leads to a commodity that's rare.

A mother who loves,
Who sacrifices and endures.
One who believes you can do anything,
Holds a heart of gold, that's pure.

A sibling that comforts,
Who makes you laugh, and helps you to be tough.
One who understands, and shares your dreams,
Encompasses a diamond in the rough.

A spouse who's loyal,
Who trusts, and doesn't embrace lies.
One who respects you, and admires what you do,
Is where you'll find a priceless prize.

Family is a treasure,
That I pray all will find.
All these things are found in its splendor,
So, leave your map behind.

Love Rearranges

We've all had our day, where we could say,
We were quite romantic.
But as the years go by, we forget how to try,
And we become quite pedantic.

We've all had a night, where everything felt right;
Where we knew what it was to swoon.
But that was before, we heard our lover's snore;
And now we howl at the moon.

We've all had a taste of a life with no haste;
We remember how long, days used to feel.
Then we pass thirty, and the kids think we're nerdy;
But that after work kiss from "lovey" we still steal.

We all have stretches where life plays out in sketches:
From paying bills, to ending fights,
We do our best to handle the rest;
The broken hearts, and night lights.

From young romance, to the kid's high school dance,
Our relationships rearrange.
From taking loves leap, to getting no sleep,
There's nothing we would change.

Love's Adventure

Love's adventure,
Has a destination unclear.
You step on the road, carrying your thoughts,
Tentatively strapped with doubt and fear.

Then you reach a path,
Unbeaten and unexplored.
You uncover feelings once hidden,
Admiration you ignored.

You journey on,
Towards your heart's desire.
Sometimes your feet get cold,
But your yearning burns like fire.

Then you go to battle,
As, "all is fair in love and war."
You fight on, and your resolve is strong,
Hoping to be the one they adore.

The expedition concludes,
In a destination undetected.
But when love's venture becomes your adventure,
Your swept off to places unexpected.

Remember

Do you remember,
When life was new?
When your mind wasn't jaded,
And your heart was open and true?

Do you recall,
The feeling that you got;
When your feet hit that summer sand,
And you ran laughing and yelling, "Hot, Hot!?"

Can you remember,
That initial ice cream cone?
When things tasted better,
And you learned to ride that bike on your own?

Can you recall,
The feeling of that first kiss?
As if life had been revealed,
And you wondered, what else did I miss?

Do you remember,
When that note in class came your way?
You tried to read it all before the teacher saw,
So, detention was delt on another day.

Do you recall,
Starting your life?
When all you owned, was pre-owned,
And anything was possible, even the strife?

Have you forgotten,

When life was new?
Has it slipped your mind,
When your heart was open and true?

CHAPTER 3

EXPERIENCE BRINGS GROWING

Personal Prison

Locked within myself,
I cannot find the key.
I curl up inside this place,
And sometimes venture to see.

The world looks different.
From inside here,
My cares are kept secret,
And my only friend is fear.

I sometimes see the light,
Till life makes me grieve.
I contemplate escape,
But I know I cannot leave.

For this is my purpose,
To cope with all this strife.
My resolution is swift,
But my sentence is for life.

Will You?

Today you are here,
Though will you be tomorrow?
Will you be feeling glad;
Or will you feel sorrow?

Will you be rich,
Or will you be poor?
Will you be healthy,
Or will regrets leave you sore?

Today you are here,
But the future you do not know.
So, will you be present in the present
Or remain in past woes?

Forgotten

Time shows its signs,
Of those you forgot,
Faces and distant places,
Of those you never sought.

These are adventures you didn't venture,
Stones left unturned,
Secrets of living, love, and giving,
That you could have learned.

These are the ones, the daughters and the sons,
You pass along the way,
Maybe you say "Hi," as you walk by,
But they had so much more to say.

These are the forgotten whose friendship can be
gotten,
If the time you will find,
To take a seat and prepare to meet,
This thing we call kind.

A Wild Life

Living in this wild life,
You learn how to adapt to;
The world that is, a jungle out there,
So, you can return to your private zoo.

You start your day in mostly the same way,
By catching your co-worker's glair.
It's that Lenore, who works up on four,
And in the morning, she is a bear.

Your day goes along, and everything's going wrong.
Your head is in a fog.
The boss says, "pick-up the pace." Like it's some kind
of a race;
And you realize, "he's working me like a dog!"

Begrudgingly, you work faster, but it's still a disaster.
And you mutter a word that isn't Merry;
Which is heard by Curt, who lives for all the dirt.
Now he's going to sing like a canary.

The day continues on, and you're ready to be gone;
To make that Five o'clock escape.
But you see it is only 3,
And this place is going ape.

You settle yourself down, but still you wear a frown,
Thinking, "this day is so uncool."
When you're cornered by Sue, who never listens to
you;
Because, she's stubborn as a mule.

You say, "take care!" As you flee for the stairs,
Like one of "hell's bats."
Then you see Bob, who got promoted, for not doing his
job.
Because he lands on his feet like a cat.

Finally, it's Five! And you've survived.
On to the car and some classic rock.
Saying, "see you later alligator,"
And not, "after 'while, you crock."

Wondering Within

I drift off to dream,
On a cloudless day.
Falling into wonder,
Where I can be who I may.

In a blast, I'm in the past,
With Doc and Marty McFly,
Reliving former mistakes, paths I shouldn't take.
Then, it's "back to the future," to reflect on why.

Suddenly, in a galaxy far, I'm Luke Skywalker, flying
at this death star.
My heart is pounding out of my chest;
But I feel this force guiding my course,
And I'm going to give it my best.

Before too long, I'm enormous, I'm King Kong!
On a rooftop, I stand tall.
Swatting at planes like ants, those who say I can't;
And I refuse to fall.

Then magically, whoa, I'm tiny! I'm Froto.
Gazing up at Mount Doom.
It looks like a tough road; and I'm carrying a heavy
load,
But I can overcome the gloom.

Then without cause, I'm ripped away to Oz.
Like Dorothy, I begin to roam.
Hoping to make a few friends, to help me in the end,
Find that place I call home.

Dreams it seems, are what lie between;
What is hoped for, and what you do.
Because you can free, what you can be,
By simply wondering within you.

Ride of Life

I sink into the seat,
I turn the key,
Ready to start life,
But where do I want to be?

I throw it into drive,
And press on the gas,
I see familiar sights,
I never thought I'd pass.

On the road and running,
To where I don't know,
Looking for guidance,
To tell me where to go.

A detour up ahead,
With my worrying, wondering to where?
My road rage emerges,
Saying this isn't fair.

I arrive in a place,
That wasn't expected,
No signs to tell where I am,
My journey redirected.

So, I motor on through,
As I learn,
You find the right way again,
Even when things turn.

I'm cruising along fine,

Then an accident stops me in my tracks,
While I pause,
I reflect on what my trip so far lacks.

My destination is in the distance,
And now I know the way,
But I've decided to slow it down,
And relish the ride each day.

A Bitter Waste

I strain to contain,
The feeling that I feel;
Like I was meant for more,
But dealt a lousy deal.

It's too late to be great!
My moment has passed me by!
I've been skipped, somehow stripped,
And I want to know why?!?

Why no one let me dance, or gave me a chance,
To have my day in the sun?
Where I'm better than you, show what I can do!
Silence the mouths of everyone!

But as I felt these things, time flew on wings.
Except, I didn't accept,
That a person's years, can be lost in tears,
If bitterness, is all you've kept.

A Fair-Weather Friend

Clouds roll in, and anxiety begins,
Doubt has come to darken my day.
Thunder shakes and anger makes,
Everything foggy, I must say.

Tears fall like rain, to wash away the pain,
I've been covered in.
It's still a damp ache, but I'm feeling I can take,
My life back again.

Then my head fills with snow, and regret lets me know,
Life's storm can be cold and unkind.
But the clouds are lifting now, and I know somehow,
I can break these ties that bind.

Then comes the sun, and a brighter day has begun,
To warm my heart, and allow me, to be me.
Because a bad day can send, a fair-weather friend,
If you let it be.

Contested, No...Con-PETS-ted

To the sayings that are cute, and to others that weirdly
suit;
To ones we have up our sleeve.
Where logic isn't strict, and pets contradict;
Those phrases we give and receive.

When we receive what we can't believe,
We say, "Don't look a gift horse in the mouth."
So how can we believe, and feel we're not deceived?
When we read those lips and hear it, "straight from the
horse's mouth."

When there's no hurry, and no need to worry,
We say we're "free as a bird," on our own.
But when time is rushing by, we no longer want to fly,
As we try to "kill two" of those "birds with one stone."

When marriage is good, and works as it should,
It's "puppy love" for us, and our spouse.
But when things go bad, and we know we're had,
We're unhappy, as we find ourselves in that "dog
house."

When we don't know what to say, and words fail us in
every way,
A "cats got our tongue."
So how can we speak, and make anger peak,
If a "catty comment" is slung?

To the sayings that are cute, and to all that weirdly
suit,

To those we have "up our sleeve."
Where logic isn't strict, and pets contradict,
The phrases we give and receive.

Persistence of the Distance

Welcome to the space, a magical place,
Where dreams are sought.
Welcome to the battleground, where agony is found,
Where the greatest wars are fought.

Welcome to the zone, where you're all alone,
Where decision holds hands with desire.
Welcome to the soul, of your control,
Where calculations are cold, and passion is on fire.

Welcome to the chain, that holds, yet is strained,
Where wrath, and forgiveness pull.
Welcome to the stage, where experience meets age,
Where one's youthful ambition, is never full.

Welcome to the hive, where you're alive,
Where all of these play their part.
Welcome, to the persistence of the distance,
Between your head, and your heart.

CHAPTER 4

TIME IS FOREVER FLOWING

A Film "Real"

This picture in my mind, is easy to find,
When I decide to stop.
I close my eyes, and to my surprise,
It starts from the top.

This picture in my mind, can relive time,
Anytime I choose.
I just hit play, and I'm back in the day;
When those I've lost, I didn't lose.

This picture in my mind, is really very kind,
In every single way.
I just press pause for any cause,
And in my happiest state I stay.

The picture in my mind, can also rewind,
To memories I wish to see.
I push recall and I witness them all,
Faces who've loved me.

This picture in my mind, never seems to bind,
What I desire to do.
I flick fast forward, and move on toward,
Anytime I want to.

The State of Mind

How do you pick up the threads;
Of an old life;
When the world throws you,
With all its strife?

How do you relive;
Years gone by?
When hopes are reborn,
And old dreams die?

How do you change;
To realize a youthful goal?
You turn back your mind,
And allow fate to take control.

A Festive Feel

It's here again,
That wonderful time of year,
When we all deck those halls,
And are filled with holiday cheer.

It's here again,
That magical, excitable glow,
In children's eyes, full of surprise,
As Christmas Trees stand watch in windows.

It's here again,
That undeniable festive feel,
When hams are bought, and we are caught,
With that warm homemade cookie, we had to steal.

It's here again,
That whimsical wintery time,
When "Frosty" lives and "Santa" gives,
All those presents, "Hey that's mine!"

It's here again,
That families reunite,
With children's roars and in-law's snores,
We sing for a "Silent Night."

It's here again,
That we gather round our tables near,
Where we thank God above for Christ and his love,
And for all those we hold dear.

Yesterdays

Some study their now,
And long to be,
Somewhere else,
Where they can find free.

Some yearn to return,
To yesterdays, so.
While others exist today,
Wishing they could let go.

But yesterdays are meant for memories,
And today is no day to quit.
Because this is the day the lord hath made,
And we should rejoice in it.

Till Time Stands Still

Till time unwinds, but somehow binds.
All who live to witness its ticks,
It brings, it takes, it destroys, it makes.
Till death has come, and what you've done, sticks.

Time endures, yet somehow implores.
All who live to hear, it's tocks,
Its constant, it changes, its rigid, it rearranges.
Till death has come, to claim the sum, of your clock.

Time steals, though somehow appeals,
To all who live to touch its hands.
Its past you lose, its present you choose,
Till, still, it stands.

Now and Then

I look at now, and ask myself how,
Did we ever get to this?
People divided, and judgements decided,
How can anyone want hatred to persist?

I look at then, and wonder when,
Did we begin to self-defeat?
Was intolerance to be blamed, or was ignorance added
to our shame?
Why does history have to repeat?

I look at now, and ask myself how,
Did we allow chaos to take place?
Where some welcome grief, and most have no belief,
In God or his grace?

I look at then, and wonder when,
Did we choose sin, instead of an eternal home?
Did it reside, when we cast Christ aside;
And chose to do things on our own?

Spoiler Alert

I sit right down,
And watch this story unfold,
But I'm already grinning,
Because its happy ending has already been told.

I see all the smiles,
That filled that familiar place,
I hear all the laughs and voices,
That sealed that time and space.

I play back the memories,
Of that blessed day,
Bringing to life those that are gone,
To relive love in my own way.

This film is too short,
And I know the end is near,
Because I have to wipe the tears away,
When love and pain's credits appear.

Time Tells

Time has seasons
And they turn.
You live through a few
And then you learn.

Time is carried off
Like a passing summer breeze;
You hope to feel it
And enjoy the moments you seize.

Time changes
Like an autumn skyline.
One day its ordinary,
While the next its sublime.

Time fades,
Like footprints in the snow.
You hold its memories,
So, they always show.

Our time is quick,
Like spring's living wonder.
So, appreciate its beauty,
Even through the rain and thunder.

Not Enough Time

I'll pay you for your time,
Is something that we say.
Should we put a price on consideration?
Should we encourage payment to be this way?

Time makes fools of us all,
Is something we are told.
So, hurry up and live it up,
Don't bother to learn as you grow old?

Thank you for your time,
Is gratitude that we give.
Shouldn't we express our pleasure,
When someone chooses to unselfishly live?

Take the time for others,
In heart and deed.
Make the time to put God first,
And in eternity you'll have all the time you need.

A Fork

We walk the path of time,
Towards a horizon we can't see.
We blindly feel our way through life,
But is that how it has to be?

Are we reaching for love;
Or holding on to wrath?
Are we content to stumble in darkness;
Or look for light to guide our path?

Do we have to remain lost;
Or lose precious years?
Do we have to wonder death, then what;
Or live forever in fear?

Are we early in our journey;
Or is the hour late?
Are we walking the wide and wicked way;
Or on a path narrow and straight?

CHAPTER 5

LOSING WILL TEST YOUR MIGHT, FAITH WILL SET IT RIGHT

Holding On

This is the hand,
That I choose to hold,
Through good or bad,
To warm when cold.

This is the hand,
I held onto,
The day you took my breath,
When you said, "I do."

This is the hand,
That clasped mine,
Reassured me I'm okay,
Reminded me I'm fine.

This is the hand,
I grabbed to be steady,
The one that won't let go,
Until I'm ready.

This is the hand,
I embrace as we pray,
The one I grip,
As I ask you to stay.

This is the hand,
I placed the ring on,
The one I held,
Until it was gone.

Without

I miss you,
And it seems unfair.
To conquer life's feats; to find an empty seat,
Because you're not there.

I miss you,
And it seems unreal,
To not hear your voice, or be able to rejoice,
Without you, it's surreal.

I miss you,
And it seems unfit,
Like a bitter taste, or a neglected embrace,
It hurts more than I admit.

I miss you,
And it seems unbelievable,
You've missed who I became, and it's not the same,
Without you inconceivable.

I miss you still,
And I know it's unwise,
To dwell in this way, because I know you'd say,
Love never dies.

No Goodbyes

How do you say goodbye;
When you yearn to say hello?
How can you make friends with silence;
Or learn to let go?

How do you resume life;
When death has taken your love?
How do you presume to forget;
When it's all you think of?

How do you get back;
To a time where things are good?
How do you move forward;
To where it feels like it could?

How do you overcome;
When down is all you've been?
You live up to a Godly life,
So, in Heaven, it's "Hello, again."

Recall for All

Here's to the fallen,
Those who've gone on before,
To the beacons that beckon my best,
And remind that I can be more.

Here's to the heroes,
Those loved and admired,
To the teachers who've taught,
And live on to inspire.

Here's to the righteous
Those faithful and just,
To the examples that echo,
Of tolerance and trust.

Here's to my God,
The one who gave all.
A son on a cross, to atone for souls lost,
So, all can hear the call.

Under You

I sit down in this place, it's hot, it's awful, okay a
disgrace,
But it suits me well.
I know most don't believe, and themselves they
deceive,
Ah, if only the dead could tell.

But let's stay on task, who am I you ask?
Well, you know my name.
I'm the one you'll see if your life is found ungodly,
But don't worry, I treat everyone the same.

I'm fair, I'm firm, and you'll only eternally burn.
Forever, I'll be your best friend.
When sitting in this spot, you really experience a lot,
Quite a unique blend.

I peer from here, and it's so clear.
As I watch what you do,
I laugh at your trust, your selfishness, your lust;
From this place under you.

I hear you lie, gossip and try,
To be more prestigious than most,
But as you chase, a smile crosses my face,
Because time you waste, until I'm your host.

I see you kill, rape, yet still;
You have no concern about me.
You think you have power, just wait till the hour;
When no mercy you'll see.

Yes, I witness you sin, and can't help but grin.
You make my job so easy.
That's right, don't be enticed by God or Christ,
And don't read the Bible, it's cheesy.

Oh, I'll root you on till your dead and gone.
Stay ignorant to God and live like you do.
Forget the cost, if your soul is lost,
And join me in this place under you.

This is a sequel to the poem: Under the Blue, from my first book, Poetry For Thought: A Tale of Life, Copyright 2020.

Faith

Faith is the substance of things hoped for,
The evidence of things not seen.
With God all things are possible,
If only you will glean.

Faith without works is dead,
So put your hand to the plow.
Don't look back,
Or you'll be found unfit when you bow.

God so loved the world,
That he gave his only son.
So, they that believe, and are baptized,
May be saved everyone.

Christ was that beloved son,
Who went to prepare us a place.
Where God will wipe away all tears,
And all shall behold true grace.

Our Father

I'm the Father,
That doesn't call you "Hun,"
But I know how many hairs are on your head,
Yes, every single one.

I'm the father,
That you don't call "Dad,"
But I know your every struggle,
Every bad day you've had.

I'm the father,
That doesn't call, or text on a phone,
But you have my word, and your prayers are always
heard,
I promise you'll never be alone.

I'm the father,
That doesn't send a card, nor a letter,
But I sent a savior, to forgive your sins,
Isn't that much better?

I'm the father,
That you can't see, hug, or greet,
But if your found worthy when your life is over,
In a heavenly home you and I will meet.

A Walk to Remember

I'm beside you now, and wondering how,
You could ever carry that cross?
I feel your pain, your hurt, your shame.
As you stumble to hold that albatross.

Then we reach the place, the time, the space,
Where your grace is truly shown.
They nail you down, you scream, they pound,
And laugh as you groan.

To the air you are lifted, your breath taken, your body
shifted,
As sacrifice was given birth.
You could've called 10,000 strong, to save yourself, to
right the wrong;
Instead of suffering alone, between Heaven and Earth.

This is the scene that is set, emotions that I get;
When I read through.
I'm right there beside, your love is my guide.
And all I can whisper, is THANK YOU.

Paroled

I look at this place, and I see no trace,
Of the person I once was.
I reminisce on now, and ask myself how;
But I know it's because…

My faith was locked, despite God's knock.
I didn't worry what he would think.
So, I continued living small, and losing all;
But that was still, just a link…

In the chain, of binding pain,
That I was shackled in,
Where my soul, would never be whole,
And life would, eternally end in sin.

Then one day, I was shown the way,
By opening up this book.
Like a key, it filled the hole in me,
And I was free to discover, the love I forsook.

I was given parole, and a new goal;
I'm told for good behavior.
If I do my part, my life will truly start,
In heaven, with my savior.

Decision Point

I feel the heat, sitting in this seat,
Week after week,
Knowing what's true, and what I need to do,
Though, I am afraid to speak.

The time has come again, as we all begin,
To take our feet and stand.
My heart is pacing, my mind is racing,
As we sing about a promise land.

So, my heart wins the fight, and I can feel that now is
right,
As I make my way towards the isle.
I tell myself I can, as I proceed to scan,
All those rows stretching for a mile.

With "Just a step, only a step,"
I feel vulnerable, yet innocent like a lamb;
But as I moved ahead, joy overcame me instead,
Because I knew, I'd be accepted, "Just as I am."

I reach the front, ready to confront,
All my sins, and things I've done.
I smile at the preacher, saying today you are a reacher,
As I confess, I've "heard and believe," before everyone.

You see, "I counted the cost if my soul should be lost,"
And I didn't like the conclusion I came to.
I was baptized, so heaven could be my prize,
And it's also waiting for you.

About the Author

Hello to all once more, wishing to explore;
The life of this "Average Joe."
I hope to proclaim and also explain,
Additional things you didn't know.

When last we talked, I had just begun to walk,
The path of authoring a book.
So, we rewound the clock and went around the block,
As we gave my upbringing a look.

This time we begin the tale, after I've set sail,
On the ocean that is a writing career.
It isn't smooth sailing, but a journey meant for
prevailing,
Through excitement, heartache, and fear.

For those who didn't read, I'll bring you up to speed.
I'm legally blind, but this isn't a story of grim;
It just gives you perception on this voyage's direction,
When all you see is dim.

My first work released in 2020. It had been exactly 20,
Years since I began to write.
For fifteen of those, no publisher chose,
To give my dream flight.

You're probably saying why, did it stink? And that's
logical to think.
But the answer is no.
You see, they thought my disability was a liability;

Or they wanted me to pay thousands to pass go.

So, I thought, on with the rest, I gave it my best.
And my work laid in a folder collecting dust.
But as my dreams were falling; a preacher's life came
calling.
I guess God had a plan that I didn't trust.

I spent years teaching, baptizing, and reaching;
Till my Aunt told me, "A Christian publisher wants a
book."
I thought, what do I have to lose? As I dusted off
courage's shoes.
And one submission was all it took.

For CPH to say, "you're now an author today."
My breath was stolen by an unseen thief.
The words seemed surreal, but I knew they were real;
Because grace comes from God's love, and our belief.

Since then, I still have to grin,
When I hear a story of how my book has helped
someone.
It's moved some to cry, others to laugh, but most to
live and try.
This is my reward, when it's fun.

Life's journey is jointly shared, but it's crosses are
uniquely bared.
So, lift yours up, when the world says you won't.
Climb life's ladder, to obtain what matters,
And never decide that your dreams don't.

Now I hope you know, more about this "Average Joe;"

The journey I took to be addressing you.
With a twenty-year smile, I'm telling you it was
worthwhile.
As I say goodbye, and God Bless, from book number
two.

Poetry
for
Thought
A Tale of Life
Derrick Stephens

www.ingramcontent.com/pod-product-compliance
Lightning Source LLC
Chambersburg PA
CBHW071502130726
47997CB00006B/2423